Original title:
The Great Life Debate: Meaning or Meme?

Copyright © 2025 Creative Arts Management OÜ
All rights reserved.

Author: Riley Donovan
ISBN HARDBACK: 978-1-80566-210-5
ISBN PAPERBACK: 978-1-80566-505-2

## The Weight of a Giggle

A chuckle weighs a feather,
It lifts you off the ground.
When laughter's light as air,
You find joy all around.

A silly joke might flop,
Yet mirth can save the day.
With irony on top,
We dance the gloom away.

Why so serious, my friend?
Life's a jest with no intent.
Like a rubber chicken's bend,
Mirth's the best money spent.

So let the smiles abound,
In each wink and silly face.
For in laughter, truth is found,
Life's a comical embrace.

**Threads of Purpose**

We weave our dreams with yarn,
In a quilt of hopes and fears.
But what is this design?
A patchwork to hold tears?

A needle pulls at fate,
Whilst bobbles dance around.
We stitch and poke and wait,
For meaning to be found.

But friends, don't take a thread,
That's fraying at the seam.
It's best if we instead,
Embrace the goofy theme.

So wear your quirks with pride,
As patterns twist and twine.
For in this silly ride,
The flaws are just divine.

## Parody of Existence

In life's absurd ballet,
We trip on cosmic jokes.
Dance like a wild bouquet,
With mismatched socks and cloaks.

A puppet's clownish grin,
Beneath a moon-lit sky.
What's real, and where's the sin?
Just ask the laughing pie.

We're jesters in this play,
With silly hats and glee.
In laughter's grand array,
We find some clarity.

So grab your feather boa,
And prance without a care.
For in this wacky show, uh,
The punchline's always there.

## **In Search of Substance**

I searched for wisdom's fruit,
But found a rubber tree.
With each profound pursuit,
I tripped on what's not me.

Like fish upon dry land,
We flop and gasp for breath.
In this wacky wonderland,
We joke about our death.

But here's the takeaway,
Amid crazy twists and turns.
Life's not just work and play,
But dancing as it burns.

So when the quest gets tough,
Just laugh and take a snack.
For meaning's not enough,
If joy's the thing we lack.

## Mosaic of Meaning

In a world where cats wear hats,
We ponder life among the sprats.
Do we seek depth or a quick delight,
As we scroll memes deep into the night?

The wise old sage eats pizza with glee,
Sipping soda, pondering what's free.
Is purpose found in laughter or plight?
Or is it just how we view the light?

Each TikTok dance, each viral shake,
When we laugh, do we wake or break?
To find the truth in giggles or grins,
Is the meaning lost in hilarious sins?

A jester juggles thoughts in the air,
With punchlines that boldly declare.
Life's a joke wrapped in layers so bright,
Is the punchline the point, or a meme on the site?

**Vibrations of Vitality**


Life's a circus, full of gags,
Where wisdom wears its tattered rags.
We leap through hoops of joy and woe,
Chasing truth in the laughs we sow.

Bubblegum dreams and jellybeans,
Exist in worlds of what-ifs and seems.
Is it the giggle or what's behind?
The secrets we keep or the jokes we find?

In memes we trust, but are they our guide?
As we ride this rollercoaster wide.
Are we just puppets on a string of fun,
Or is there meaning in the laughter spun?

So let's go dancing, twirling about,
In the chaos of chuckles, there's never a doubt.
Seeking value within the jest,
In the game of life, we're all just blessed!

## Reality's Comedy

In a world of virtual dreams,
Laughter spills at the seams.
Chasing likes, we play our parts,
But who's the clown, and who's got smarts?

A cat in a hat? A dog with a tie?
We scroll through the nonsense, oh me, oh my!
Life's a stage, and we all are cast,
Finding joy in the absurdity, quite a blast!

## Finding Essence in Irony

In the quest for wisdom, we trip and fall,
Stumbling over hashtags, we giggle and crawl.
The deeper we search for meaning so bright,
The funnier it gets, what a curious sight!

With memes that preach what they barely know,
We laugh at ourselves, it's quite the show.
Irony speaks in clever disguise,
As we grasp at the truth that twists and flies!

## The Dance of Meaning

We tango with thoughts, both lofty and small,
Tripping on puns while we waltz down the hall.
Each step carries weight, a playful charade,
As we whirl through this life, our worries allayed.

In the rhythm of giggles, we spin round and round,
Searching for wisdom where folly is found.
Twisters of meaning, we're all in a trance,
Finding grace in our blunders — let's laugh and dance!

## Laughter as Logic

They claim wisdom's heavy, a burden to bear,
But laughter is light, it's the ultimate air.
Reasoning's fun when it tickles the brain,
Forget all the answers, just chuckle at pain!

In the absurdity, we find our own light,
A joke for our troubles, and all feels just right.
So gather your giggles, embrace the bizarre,
For laughter's the compass — the best guiding star!

## Meme as Metaphor

In the land of cat photos,
Wisdom is just a joke,
Pixels dance, truth elopes,
With laughter, we invoke.

Scroll and tap, night flies by,
Philosophy in a GIF,
Meaning hides in the sly,
A viral, chuckling myth.

Memes are dreams, dreams are memes,
Life's a never-ending feed,
What's sincere? Oh, it seems,
Popularity is the creed.

In a world of endless trends,
Thoughts become quickfire quips,
Forget defense, make amends,
Each click propels our trips.

## The Quest for Authenticity

Searching for the real deal,
In a sea of filters bright,
Is that smile yours to steal?
Or just pixels in the light?

Posting brunch with avocado,
Insta-worthy, no despair,
Authentic or just a chateau,
Where truth hides behind the glare?

"Live your truth," the banners scream,
But who knows what that means?
As we chase the perfect dream,
While life flows in fragments' seams.

With hashtags and with likes,
We sail through our own parade,
In the circus, truth takes hikes,
And reality can fade.

## Chasing Shadows of Meaning

I chased meaning in the night,
It wore a cape, ran too fast,
A shadow tricked me in fright,
With laughter, it was outclassed.

Every riddle, every sign,
Turns into a game of tag,
"Look at me!" it writes on brine,
But meaning? It's a frayed rag.

In mirrors where we seek the clue,
Wit, wits, and quips take the lead,
Oh, how absurd life can skew,
As we ponder every deed.

So we giggle, twirl and spin,
Life's a riddle wrapped in jest,
Chasing shadows, we still win,
Finding fun in every quest.

## **Absurdity's Embrace**

In comedy lies great wisdom,
A parable wrapped in a joke,
Absurdity's the grand prism,
Through which the odd thoughts poke.

Why take life too seriously?
When clowns can teach us to laugh,
Each blunder becomes a spree,
With giggles, we map our path.

In the chaos, truth slips through,
Like butter on a hot toast,
Absurdity's our best crew,
We raise a glass, we shall boast.

Let's uproar with all our might,
As nonsense gives birth to ways,
In absurdity's warm light,
Life's a series of wild plays.

## Revelations in Ridicule

In a world of grand designs,
We ponder life's most silly signs.
Is it wisdom or a meme,
That makes us laugh or dream?

We trip on thoughts like bouncing balls,
While wisdom giggles in the halls.
With each profound, absurd debate,
We find the truth—it's just our fate!

Do cats with hats hold deep insight?
Or are we wrong to think it's bright?
In jest we seek, in laughs we dwell,
Perhaps the joke's on us as well!

So raise a toast with clinking cups,
To life's great riddles, ups, and blups!
As laughter echoes, we will cheer,
With memes, my friend, there's naught to fear!

## The Layers of Laughter

Beneath the surface, jokes reside,
Like onions, layers, we can't hide.
Is meaning packed in something sly?
Or do we laugh and wonder why?

Philosophers wear silly hats,
While pondering over glorious cats.
To laugh is wisdom, so they say,
Yet here I sit, just lost in play!

With each good quip, a truth unveiled,
In laughter, countless thoughts are hailed.
Do memes hold lessons we can share,
Or is the purpose just the air?

So gather round, let silliness flow,
For life's a circus, don't you know?
With chuckles bridging hearts and minds,
Perhaps in laughter, meaning finds!

## Unwritten Writings of Existence

In scrolls unmade, life's tales await,
With punchlines hiding 'neath the slate.
Is purpose scribbled in a joke?
Or does our laughter form the cloak?

We dance on thoughts like feet on grass,
With memes that glide and moments pass.
Awkward pauses, nervous grins,
Is that where life's true meaning spins?

From ancient scrolls to modern screens,
Our laughter weaves through all the scenes.
Shall we be jesters, wise or free?
Or just the punchline in a spree?

In whimsical quips, our joys reside,
As seriousness we set aside.
Let's pen our tales of jests and glee,
In unwritten scripts, we find our spree!

## The Essence of a Chuckle

A chuckle here, a snicker there,
Could meaning dance or even dare?
With smiles that twinkle in the night,
Is it the joke or pure delight?

With every giggle, wisdom tumbles,
As life transforms and softly fumbles.
Is truth a pun or just a glance?
Or did we miss the cosmic chance?

We question life with every jest,
In wit we search for all the best.
Is laughter key to sacred paths?
Or merely echoes of our laughs?

So let us toast to silly woes,
Embrace the jest as wisdom grows.
For in the chuckles that we share,
Perhaps life's meaning lingers there!

## Laughter's Labyrinth


In a world of endless chatter,
We ponder what really matters.
Is it love or just a snack?
Silly thoughts we can't turn back.

Searching for wisdom in the froth,
Is it truth or just a sloth?
We giggle at what we can't find,
The memes of life are truly kind.

With every scroll, we grip and scroll,
Is that wisdom or just a troll?
Life's a joke that twists and bends,
For laughter's the path that never ends.

## Tapestries of Thought

Weaving thoughts in colors bright,
Questions dance like birds in flight.
Is the answer hidden deep?
Or just a laugh that we should keep?

A meme can sparkle, shine, and glow,
While wisdom hides, you never know.
We ponder, laugh, and scratch our heads,
In a world where quips are threads.

What truly counts? The joy or jest?
We stitch together our own quest.
In this fabric, truth may fray,
But humor makes it bright and gay.

## Questions Within Quips

What's the deal with life today?
Is it serious or just play?
Each quip a puzzle, wrapped in cheer,
Do we find meaning or just veneer?

Hiding truth behind a joke,
Did you hear that? Or was it smoke?
Our laughter's the glue, tight and sweet,
Woven in banter, life's quirky beat.

Is it deep or just a phase?
We question, laugh, in a daze.
For every quip, a thought unspun,
In a world where joy is number one.

## A Banter with Being

In the café of life, we sip and chat,
Is existence real, or just a spat?
Between the sips, the giggles grow,
Life's a jest, don't you know?

Philosophers pause for a slice of pie,
While memes of memes make their reply.
We laugh at depth, it's quite absurd,
In this banter, wisdom's blurred.

So raise a glass to questions deep,
In this jest, find a laugh to keep.
What matters most, the thought or fun?
In this banquet, we savor each pun.

## Serendipity in Simulacra

In a world where laughter's key,
We chase memes in jubilee.
Life's oddities, we hold dear,
Like pigeons dancing, oh so sheer.

Late-night thoughts with friends we share,
Why is cheese a billionaire's heir?
In the chaos and the cheer,
We find strange truth and drink a beer.

**Eternal Jests**

Time travels fast with a comedy act,
Twirling jokes like a hat momentarily cracked.
Life's strange punchlines keep us on our toes,
As irony blooms like a weed that just grows.

How many paths lead to a laugh?
Is it the meme or the barista's photograph?
With fables tossed like a rolled-up sock,
We trade silly stumbles on this ticking clock.

## **A Riddle in Every Smile**

Faces grin while pondering fate,
Are we players or just bait?
Each chuckle echoes, masked surprise,
As riddles dance behind bright eyes.

With every snort and hearty guffaw,
The universe winks, 'Is this all law?'
We serve up giggles, dish out style,
Creating meaning just with a smile.

## Depth Beneath the Surface

In shallow pools of viral waves,
We dive for meaning, like playful knaves.
The profundity of a cat in a box,
Reveals secret thoughts, like grandfather clocks.

Underneath the scrolling fun,
Existential crises weigh a ton.
Yet we laugh as the memes unfold,
Searching for truths, both charming and bold.

## **Joy in Jobs of Meaning**

In a world where tasks can shine,
I asked my goldfish, what is divine?
He swam in circles, made quite a splash,
'The job's not the dream, it's the cash you'll stash!'

I wrote my resume, with flair and with flair,
Said I could juggle while breathing fresh air.
But my boss just chuckled, 'What's this all worth?'
'Just find joy in the chaos of virtual mirth!'

## The Synthesis of Significance

A peacock preens in its rainbow attire,
While pondering purpose by the old campfire.
Hummingbirds help, flitting in glee,
'It's not just a job; it's pure snazzy spree!'

So I took up knitting, and boy did I fail,
My scarf turned a mob, an alien flail.
Yet laughter erupted, we danced in delight,
For significance sometimes is just joking right!

## **Moments of Merriment**

In a coffee shop where ideas take flight,
A barista dropped foam that danced in the light.
'This cappuccino's deep, like my thoughts, you see,'
I sipped and I pondered, 'Is this just for me?'

But laughter erupted from a table nearby,
They stumbled on puns, and I couldn't deny.
In moments so silly, the essence we stake,
Is laughter in life, for our sanity's sake!

## The Philosophy of Giggles

A wise old sage with a beard like a mop,
Said, 'Life's a big riddle, now do the hop!'
With each jig and jive, he held his ground strong,
'Meaning's great, but laughter is where we belong!'

So we gathered our friends, a silly parade,
With rubber duck hats and a slip-n-slide blade.
In the chaos, we found, with glee on display,
Giggles are wisdom—our own funny way!

## **Buried Truths in Humor**

In a world where laughs collide,
Truth hides under jokes, snide.
A meme may giggle, wise and bright,
While meaning trolls just out of sight.

Peeling layers, what a mess,
Finding truths in silliness.
Digging deeper, what's the score?
A giggle chorus, evermore.

But what if humor leads the way?
Can joy outshine the mundane gray?
With every chuckle, wisdom's spun,
A paradox, a riddle fun.

So let's embrace this wacky quest,
Where laughter's truly at its best.
We'll dance through memes and meanings wide,
In this jesting world, we'll take our ride.

## Doodles of Deepness

A doodle sketch, so carefree,
Yet hidden depths, can't you see?
A scribble laughing, truths unfold,
Meaning's there, but oh-so-bold.

With crayon colors, bright and wild,
We draw out wisdom, like a child.
Silly shapes, a clown's facade,
Yet in the chaos, there's a nod.

So let's embrace this silly art,
Where giggles mix with a thoughtful heart.
Each line a jolt, each curve a cheer,
In our doodles, life's quite clear!

From meme to meaning, a twisty fate,
An artful dance, let's celebrate!
In the nonsense, truth's compass gleams,
Drawing laughter from our dreams.

## Jigsaw of Joy

A puzzle piece, a quirky smile,
Joy's jigsaw, it's worth the while.
Each fragment holds a sneaky clue,
To meanings that are bright and new.

Here's a meme, oh what a sight,
Twisted truths and pure delight!
We fit them in, oh what a game,
In this chaos, joy's the same.

Can meaning hide in goofy grins?
Or does it dance where laughter spins?
The pieces swirl, the laughter shows,
In every dip, the joy just flows.

So let's create this playful mess,
With every piece, we'll find success!
A jigsaw life, absurd and bright,
Where memes and meaning both unite.

## Spectrum of Seriousness

A silly spectrum, jokes abound,
Seriousness, it's spinning round.
From memes that tingle, truths that sting,
In this circus, we find our swing.

A serious laugh or a funny frown,
In every shade, let's not back down.
With every quip, a lesson learned,
In laughter's glow, a fire burned.

What's the meaning behind the jest?
Who knew the punchline could be the best?
In shades of humor, truth will gleam,
A serious laugh, life's wildest dream.

So come along this quirky ride,
Through every meme and meaning tide.
In this spectrum, let's all cheer,
For life's a giggle, let's make it clear!

**Truths Held Lightly**

In a world of tweets and tales,
We juggle wisdom with our scales.
A meme, a laugh, a clever pun,
Can sometimes shine like morning sun.

What's deep, they ask, what counts as true?
Is it the wise or morning dew?
With giggles shared around a screen,
Do we find meaning in the keen?

When hashtags trend and thoughts collide,
Are we just surfing on the tide?
The laughter echoes, light and free,
Dancing there in absurdity.

So hold your truths like summer leaves,
They flutter down, as memory weaves.
In playful jest, let's find our way,
Through serious thought and humor's sway.

## The Dance of Depth and Delight

A philosopher walks into a bar,
Sips his drink, and ponders far.
He fumbles with his deep intent,
While memes come flying, simply bent.

What's profound? What's just a riff?
He smiles; it seems he's got the gift.
For between the wise and silly lies,
A world that chuckles, never cries.

With every scroll, new gems arise,
In laughter's arms, we theorize.
A nugget of truth or just some fun?
In this grand dance, we're all spun.

So grab your thoughts, twirl them around,
In this light-hearted space, we're bound.
For depths and delights do intertwine,
In playful banter, something divine.

## Fragmented Philosophies

A thought so grand, it trips a light,
Falls flat on memes, what a sight!
Reality bends, perception made,
In every jest, our worries fade.

Socrates might say, "Know thyself,"
But lost in memes, is joy the wealth?
With every quip, we navigate,
Complex thoughts in simple slate.

From deep ideas to cat-filled lore,
We ponder life while we explore.
A quote, a laugh, a viral thread,
Can spin the mind, from dread to spread.

So gather close, in this charade,
Laugh at the truth we have conveyed.
In fragments, we find our way to see,
Life's absurdities, wild and free.

## **Heartbeats of Humor**

A scientist says, "Life's a joke,"
As laughter bursts like morning smoke.
With every beat, the heart will play,
In silly rhythms, fun's underway.

With wisdom spoken in a jest,
We seek the truth, but humor's best.
In every chuckle, mystery lies,
In lightness found, the spirit flies.

Philosophy wrapped in laughter's charm,
Can keep the world from doing harm.
In memes and joy, we find our groove,
As deep thoughts dance, our souls will move.

So clutch your heart, let humor reign,
In this wild game, there's much to gain.
Through laughter, truths we might unveil,
In each heartbeat, let joy prevail.

# **Pixels and Philosophy**

In pixels we trust, but who truly knows,
Are they wisdom or just quirky shows?
My cat just posted a selfie with flair,
Does that make her deep? Or just quite rare?

We scroll and we swipe through wisdom and memes,
Searching for truth in our digital dreams.
A philosopher's quote in a comic strip,
Is it thought-provoking or just a fun quip?

A dog in a hat pondering life's big schemes,
Debating existence while pulling at seams.
The clouds share their thoughts on comedic bliss,
With every odd hashtag, we laugh and dismiss.

So here's to the pixels that lighten the load,
Life's silly moments, on this wild road.
With each witty post, a small truth we find,
In pixels and laughter, there's meaning entwined.

## **Jests of the Soul**

Does a joke have a heart? Or just punchlines tossed,
Are the laughs of the world worth all the cost?
A penguin in tux, with a quip to impart,
Leaves us chuckling and scratching our heart.

In laughter we wander, like kids on a swing,
Finding the depth in the simplest thing.
Philosophers chuckle from far out of sight,
As memes bring the truth with a wink and delight.

Is life a grand joke, or a jest we all share?
With each belly laugh, do we boldly declare?
An avocado's wisdom wrapped up in green,
Tells us to guacamole our thoughts in between.

So here's to the jesters who wiggle and dance,
Chasing the meaning in life's funny chance.
If humor's the answer, let's giggle and troll,
For the world's simply better when teased by the soul!

## Truth in the Absurd

In the absurdity, truth wears a hat,
A chicken debates with a wise-looking cat.
They ponder existence over fancy cheese,
Both baffled by life, yet sharing a tease.

A toaster sings songs while the kettle just grins,
Could the secrets of life lie in breakfast spins?
We seek for the meaning in odd little quirks,
While the universe chuckles and antics perks.

The worm wears a tie, quite dressed for the show,
Arguing life from the soil down below.
What is the purpose? The crowd is unsure,
Is it all just a game, or an answer so pure?

So embrace the absurd in its quirky array,
For sometimes the laughter is really the way.
With a wink and a giggle, we plunge into bliss,
Where truth isn't logic, but a sweet, silly kiss.

## **Playful Paradox**

A paradox dances with a riddle in tow,
It flips through the pages of life's wondrous show.
Is a fish in a hat truly wise or confused?
Is laughter the answer or merely enthused?

The sun takes a nap while the moon's in a race,
Yet every odd moment has its perfect place.
A pickle debates if it's sour or sweet,
In this wacky affair, we all feel replete.

The clouds take a selfie, preparing for fame,
While rain drops like tears in this humorous game.
With giggles and grins, we skip through the day,
Each twist in the tale is a reason to play.

So let's toast to the playful, the weird in between,
For life's not a puzzle, but a comical scene.
In paradox's grip, let's all find a spark,
With laughter our light in the revelry's dark.

## **Dreams Wrapped in Pixels**

In a world of filters and bright hues,
We ponder if life's just a game we choose.
Is it memes that make us laugh and gleam?
Or deeper wonders found in a dream?

Scroll through feeds, catch a glimpse of bliss,
But beneath the laughter, something's amiss.
Is a cat in a hat the height of fun?
Or is there more to life than a viral pun?

Each like we get feels like time well spent,
Yet the heart knows truths the pixels omit.
Dancing in shadows, we mimic the trends,
But the laughter fades, just a means to an end?

So here's to the chaos of screens we chase,
Finding meaning in this digital space.
With jokes on repeat and puns on a roll,
We search for the essence, the depth of our soul.

## Whispers of Reality

In a world where laughter is pixelated,
And wisdom's often underrated.
Do we chase the likes or seek the truth?
In silly hashtags, is freedom uncouth?

Scrolling through memes with joy and despair,
We question existence hidden in flair.
Is a selfie a story or just a facade?
When the laughter's done, do we feel like a fraud?

Reality whispers while giggles explode,
Life's a weird puzzle, a quirky code.
Do we trade the depth for a fleeting grin?
Or find joy in memes where the laughter begins?

So let's raise a glass to the wittiest lines,
To the funny, the bizarre, the break from designs.
In the mix of it all, let's dance and debate,
For meaning and memes together create!

## **A Canvas of Thoughts**

Brush strokes of laughter on a canvas wide,
We paint our lives as we laugh and slide.
Do we splash some meaning or pixel a scream?
As we question life through each vibrant meme?

Every post a glimpse of this funny parade,
Yet deeper reflections are often delayed.
A joke can enlighten, or so we assume,
While wisdom might lurk on the edge of a zoom.

With colors of humor, we sketch out our fate,
We scribble our whims, then we ponder our state.
Is a chuckle enough in this humorous race?
Or do we need depth alongside our wild chase?

So let's laugh at the absurd, embrace the jest,
In a world full of pixels, we search for the rest.
For amidst every meme, a truth might appear,
That life's not just funny, but worthy of cheer!

## Searching for Substance

In the realm of memes, we search for delight,
But is laughter enough in this ongoing fight?
As we scroll and chuckle, we glance at the void,
Wondering if meaning is being destroyed.

Each silly video, a momentary high,
Yet the hunger for substance is always nearby.
Are we laughing too hard, or just trying to cope?
Or is finding the funny our only true hope?

Do the hashtags we follow hold secrets inside?
Or just empty echoes where our dreams reside?
As we post, do we ponder what's real and what's fake?
Or is joy the pursuit till the last laughter break?

So let's toast to the fun, to the giggles we share,
In a world bound by pixels, we'll boldly declare.
For laughter's a treasure, just may not suffice,
In this quirky adventure, we'll keep rolling the dice!

## Parables of the Playful

In the land of giggles, the wise men meet,
They argue over meaning, with jokes as their treat.
A cat in a hat claims he knows the score,
While the dog in the corner just sleeps on the floor.

Why chase your tail when you can chase a dream?
Reality's warped, or so it would seem.
With laughter as currency, they barter their thoughts,
Swapping old paradoxes for chuckles and knots.

They ponder existence while sipping on tea,
One claims he's a ghost, the other just me.
Philosophers juggling their motivational memes,
Crafting new realities like whimsical dreams.

With each punchline tossed, the crowd bursts with cheer,
Unraveling the truth, or is it just near?
In a world full of jest, do answers reside,
Or do we just giggle and take them in stride?

## Philosophy in Punchlines

Tickle my brain with your clever retorts,
In jest there's a wisdom that shines and cavorts.
A chicken crossed roads, but it was just a ruse,
To ponder life's meaning while dodging the blues.

A wink from the cosmos, a punchline divine,
'Life's but a joke,' says the old sage's line.
As the stars giggle back, we chuckle along,
Finding solace in humor, our lifelong song.

The philosophers' brawl spills into the night,
With each quip a clue, a comedic delight.
Are we jesters of fate, or fate's merry jest?
Life's existential riddle all put to the test.

Who needs a scribe when we laugh at our woes?
Each joke adds a layer, as everybody knows.
So let's raise our glasses to punchlines so sly,
For life's not a question, it's a whimsical pie!

## The Depth of Delusion

Taking a dive into the pool of confusion,
Splashing about in this grand delusion.
Do ducks quack in tongues, or is that all a jest?
To swim with such questions, now isn't that best?

As wisdom floats by on a rubbery raft,
We ponder the meaning of each silly shaft.
Behold the wise owl, with spectacles round,
Reading memes from the past, profound but unsound.

Is the secret to happiness found in a tweet?
Can a word make you dance, or move your two feet?
With laughter our lifeline, we search to align,
In a circus of truth, we each draw a line.

So join the parade of the clueless and spry,
For clarity's boring, and we're all just a tie.
With a wink and a nod, our illusions take flight,
In the depths of delusion, we laugh into the night!

## Reflections in a Laugh

Mirror, mirror, on the wall, quite amusing,
What's the meaning behind our daily cruising?
A giggle in the groove, a chuckle in stride,
In reflections of laughter, our truths do collide.

Here in the circus of thought and of jest,
Truths swap places, we attend to the rest.
A squirrel in a suit claims he knows the way,
While bunnies debate if it's night or it's day.

Do we unravel the mysteries, or just bask in delight?
Finding humor in riddles, through day and through night.
The more that we ponder, the funnier it gets,
As punchlines and wisdom engage in their bets.

So let's dance with the absurd, in laughter we thrive,
In the land of reflections, we all feel alive.
For while we might search for that magical beam,
Life's better when wrapped in a comical dream!

## Ciphers of the Heart

In a world of hearts and memes,
We find meaning in silly schemes.
Like texting hearts with cat-shaped wings,
And pondering what true love brings.

With emojis dancing in the air,
We send our feelings everywhere.
Is love a tweet or a deep sigh?
Perhaps it's just a clever lie.

Yet on this path of memes we tread,
We laugh at things we never said.
A wink, a nudge, a playful jest,
Reveal our hearts, we're at our best.

Amidst the noise, a chuckle bright,
Finding joy in the virtual fight.
So here we are, both near and far,
Trying to decode just who we are.

## **Nuances of Nonsense**

What is sense without a giggle?
Like trying to dance but tripping a little.
We ponder life's profound displays,
While splatting cream pies in playful ways.

Theories diverse, as wobbly as jello,
Wisdom drips from a flamboyant fellow.
An argument sparked by a rubber duck,
In this nonsense, we find our luck.

Chasing thoughts that run in loops,
Like lost puppies amongst silly groups.
Is clarity hidden in tangled lines?
Or is it just a riddle with punchy pines?

So grab a meme, hold it tight,
Let laughter dance into the night.
For in chaos and silliness, we find,
The nuanced joys of a playful mind.

## The Essence of Absurdity

In a realm where logic takes a break,
We juggle thoughts like a silly snake.
Worms in suits make for fine debate,
As pizza slices on quantum fate.

Absurdities rise like dandelions,
While rationality quietly resigns.
Tickled by thoughts that touch the sky,
Can nonsense ever ask us why?

Life's comedy masks the serious stuff,
As we giggle at paths that feel so rough.
Finding truth in a chuckle or two,
Our minds become fuzzy, but that's nothing new.

With each joke, we untangle the wires,
Fanning the flames of our crazy fires.
So let's laugh loud with hearts wide open,
Embracing absurdity, the fun's unbroken.

## Luminous Laughter

From deep within our quirky core,
Emerges a light that we can't ignore.
Through giggles bright and smiles wide,
We ride the waves of humor's tide.

With every chuckle, worries fade,
A standing ovation for the knucklehead parade.
We chat about wisdom from quirky souls,
Striking poses like irreverent moles.

A belly laugh shared, a meme gone viral,
Our minds aligned in perfect spiral.
Between the laughs, truth dances near,
In every punchline, we find cheer.

So here's to laughter, our radiant art,
A joyful spark that warms the heart.
In silliness wrapped, we find our theme,
Luminous laughter, the ultimate dream.

## The Anecdote of Existence

In a world of dreams and meme-filled tales,
The search for meaning often derails.
We ponder our purpose, laugh then cry,
While cats rule the internet and pigeons fly.

Philosophers ponder in coffee shops,
While TikTok trends make wisdom drop.
Is life a joke or the punchline's chase?
Grab a laugh, wear a smile, and find your place.

So join in the banter, don't take it too hard,
Existence can be quirky, not always a guard.
From deep thoughts to memes with a cat on a chair,
Life's a circus show, but hey, who cares?

In moments of doubt, just take a quick peek,
At selfies of dogs who can't help but speak.
With every hashtag, we find our way,
Embracing the weirdness of every day.

## Whimsy and Wisdom

A squirrel in a suit declares with a grin,
"Life's a comedy, let the laughter begin!"
With memes flying by and wisdom on pause,
We dance to the rhythm of life's silly laws.

A sage once said, in a TikTok dance,
"Find meaning in memes, give your soul a chance."
So we clap and we cheer for the silly and sweet,
Finding joy in the odd, it's hard to beat.

From puns that tickle to quips that inspire,
We juggle our thoughts like a clown on a wire.
Let whimsy take over, let worries dissolve,
For what's truly wise is how we evolve.

So laugh with abandon, and meme with delight,
When life gets too serious, bring humor to light.
In this mix of the mad, we find our own key,
For the heart of existence is goofy and free.

## Catharsis in Comedy

Behind every joke lies a truth to reveal,
In laughter we heal, in chuckles we feel.
Gather 'round friends, with wit on display,
We'll ponder our lives in a light-hearted way.

A lost sock laments, 'Who'll bring me back home?'
As we search high and low, laughing while we roam.
The essence of life, a comedic ballet,
Where chaos and humor engage in a fray.

Life's absurd and it's wildly sincere,
Like a fish out of water, or a cat with no fear.
In every mishap, a lesson appears,
With laughter as armor, we conquer our fears.

So share in the folly, let laughter abound,
In the absurdity's arms, we all will be found.
With joy as our compass, we'll navigate schemes,
For the punchlines of life are the truest of dreams.

## The Texture of the Mind

In a quilt of thoughts, absurd and bright,
We patch our ideas in day and night.
Some threads hold wisdom, others just memes,
Yet every decision is stitched with our dreams.

A doodle of chaos can spark a new thought,
While pondering purpose, we often forget.
With every quirk added, our fabric expands,
Where humor meets reason with laughter in hand.

A tickle of wit can unravel the seams,
Turning questions to answers wrapped soft in beams.
So we giggle and ponder the great cosmic jest,
Finding meaning in nonsense, we humor the rest.

So embrace the textures, both quirky and fine,
From memes that confound to moments divine.
In every weird twist, we're weaving our fate,
Where laughter and wisdom both find their great mate.

## The Philosophy of Laughter

Why do we laugh, oh tell me please,
Is it to tickle the funny-boned geese?
With jokes that twist and tick-tock time,
Is humor the answer, or just a pantomime?

In a world that spins like a dizzy top,
We giggle and guffaw, we hop and bop.
A joke's a riddle wrapped in a pun,
Where logic hides, and fun's the one.

When life gets heavy, we dance and sing,
With wacky wigs and a rubber chicken fling.
Our brains may ponder, but hearts just play,
In silliness found, we light our way.

So here's to laughter, our sweet relief,
In every chuckle, we find belief.
Meaning may flit like a butterfly's wing,
But laughter's the gift that keeps us in spring.

## Life's Absurd Canvas

In a world where socks do not match,
And pizza speaks of a playful catch.
We paint with crayons, the skies are pink,
On canvases where logic starts to shrink.

What's serious faces in a clown parade,
Though life may tease, it's never delayed.
We juggle our dreams like a circus act,
In the carnival of life, that's a fact!

Finding meaning in a rubber band,
As we stretch, we also must understand.
A spatula sings when it flips a pancake,
Absurdity lives in the moves that we make.

So gather 'round for a confetti fight,
Where nonsense reigns, and joy feels right.
In a world where laughter is a bold dance,
Let silliness guide us; give it a chance.

## Silliness in Seriousness

In suits and ties, they shuffle their feet,
With spreadsheets and coffee, their minds feel elite.
But look closely now, peer beneath the guise,
A rubber chicken in their pocket lies!

With meetings scheduled from dawn to dusk,
They ponder life with a serious husk.
Yet whispers of giggles escape their lips,
Between all the checks and the data quips.

For all of the brooding and serious talk,
There's ice cream to eat on the moonlit walk.
With every stern note there's silliness near,
A pie in the face brings laughter and cheer.

So let's toast to those who juggle the two,
In a world that's quirky, where joy breaks through.
For in the mundane, the funny we find,
Laughter's the key to unburden the mind.

## Meaning's Fleeting Mirage

Chasing meaning like a cat with a mouse,
In the corners of life, in every small house.
But meaning flits by like a butterfly bright,
Leaving us giggling through day and through night.

With every deep thought, there's a punchline that stings,
Like finding lost socks that aren't from the Kings.
We ponder and wonder, while making a meme,
That plays in our heads like a raucous dream.

Oh, wisdom escapes when we wrangle the truth,
Wrapped up in ribbons of whimsical youth.
In searching for meaning, we find silly games,
Where laughter's the language that always inflames.

So when life is heavy and questions arise,
Remember the humor that often belies.
For in every quest, whether serious or fickle,
It's the laughter we share that makes hearts do a tickle.

## Existential Echoes

In a world so absurd, we ponder our roles,
Is it all just a jest, or do we play goals?
The chicken crossed streets, with a wink and a quip,
Maybe life's just a sitcom, a humorous trip.

We chase after meaning, like cats chase their tails,
While laughter erupts, in ridiculous scales.
So let's raise a toast, to confusion and glee,
In the carnival of life, come join in the spree.

What if all of existence is just one big prank?
A cosmic joke teller, at the far end of rank.
We dance on the brink, of absurdity's nest,
With punchlines and puns, we're all humor's guests.

So bring on the chuckles, the wisecrack parade,
In the theater of life, we laugh unafraid.
Because sometimes, dear friend, in the chaos and cheer,
It's the laughter that counts, as we sip on our beer.

## **Laughter in the Void**

Caught in the void, where the echoes collide,
We trip on our thoughts, and our reason gets fried.
Like socks in the dryer, we tumble and roll,
Searching for sense, in the depths of our soul.

The universe giggles, as planets align,
What's serious now? Let's declare it benign!
A cosmic comedian, with stars for a stage,
Punchlines delivered, as we turn every page.

Farts in the cosmos, a sound that rings clear,
Do they laugh up there, or just hide in fear?
With each little hiccup, we bust at the seams,
In this boundless drama, we chase after dreams.

So let's toast to the void, where nothing seems real,
With laughter as armor, we'll conquer and feel.
For in the grand scheme, what truly is fate?
A joke and a chuckle may just be our slate.

## Whispers of Significance

In the grand hall of life, with whispers of glee,
We search for the meaning, as if it might flee.
A squirrel on a branch gives a riddle to share,
Is significance born, or conjured from air?

Like jesters and kings, we play parts on this stage,
In the book of existence, we scribble a page.
A tickle of thought, a quip from the past,
Is wisdom a meme, or in laughter we last?

With gravity's pull and a buoyant surprise,
We juggle our quirks, under unblinking skies.
As we flirt with absurdity, side-split with delight,
Laughter's the anchor, in the dark of the night.

So let's crack a smile, as we dance through the haze,
With humorous riddles, we dazzle and graze.
For in this grand puzzle, where questions abound,
It's the giggles that echo, the joy we have found.

## Jokes in the Cosmos

Is the universe laughing, or just playing us fools?
We build our great castles, while dancing on stools.
In cosmic comic strips, where humor survives,
We sift through the nonsense, and seek out our vibes.

The planets are chuckling, the comets all wink,
With each little mishap, we stop and we think.
Are we just cosmic blunders, tossed 'twixt time and space?

In this slapstick adventure, we all find our place.

With humor as fuel, we soar through the night,
In the vastness of chaos, we glimpse a new light.
For meaning's a riddle, all tangled and spinny,
Yet jokes warm our hearts, like a big bowl of mini.

So gather your laughter, let's ride this great wave,
In a universe teeming with jests that we crave.
For in the end, darling, as we blink and we jest,
It's the smiles we leave, that truly are best.

## **Wit and Wisdom Collide**

In the realm of banter bold,
Where truths and jests unfold.
A sage can joke, a fool can preach,
Yet wisdom eludes when laughs are in reach.

Sarcastic quips, deep insights mesh,
A riddle's punch, a thinker's flesh.
When answers hide within a jest,
We ponder life—what's best?

Is joy a path, or just a detour?
With humor's light, we're never unsure.
So raise a glass, let laughter ring,
As we dance with memes and meaning's sting.

In wisdom's cloak, the jester hides,
Witty remarks where truth abides.
From laughter's spark, enlightenment grows,
In this funny game, everyone knows!

## Beyond the Punchline

A laugh is a gift, wrapped tight in a quip,
But what's the meaning? Just let it slip.
A sigh of relief from a wisecrack's sound,
Could it be depth that's tightly bound?

In jokers and jesters, the truth may lay,
Beneath chuckles and giggles, amid the fray.
A punchline strikes, a life's big question,
Are we just memes in a wild procession?

With each silly tale, we turn and we twist,
The essence of life—cling to or resist?
Funny as heck, yet deeply profound,
Where laughter and reason together abound.

So chuckle away at the quirky, the wild,
Who knew such thoughts could be so beguiled?
In the realm of jest, find your own way,
To mash up the math of wisdom's ballet!

## The Riddle of Reality

What is real? Is it this or that?
A meme on my screen or a joke from the cat?
As I ponder with glee, do I find some sense,
Or just chase my tail, in laugh's pretense?

Life's full of puzzles, like socks on the floor,
Each one weaves tales of "more and more."
So I ask my wise friend, sipping a brew,
"Is the riddle of life just an old meme too?"

In asking the questions, willy-nilly we stride,
A chuckle erupts from the wisdom inside.
Reality giggles, hiding away,
In the shadows of laughter, what can we say?

With humor as armor, and truth as our guide,
Let's navigate life, with chuckles beside.
For in the absurd, may the answers arrive,
With wit by our side, we're bound to survive!

## Playful Paradoxes

A pickle in a puzzle, a riddle in glee,
What's nonsense depends on who's sipping the tea.
In the land of the quirky, the wise and the mad,
The line gets a twist; it's fun to be had.

Boolean beliefs and memes in the air,
To figure 'em out, do we even care?
As we laugh at the logic, the humor not dense,
True meaning takes flight in a Google search fence.

In paradox's grip, we dance and we play,
What's serious? Just memes in a whimsical fray.
So here's to the jesters who tickle our minds,
As we flip over life, a smile it finds.

So puzzle your pals with a chuckle or two,
Pour out your wisdom with a giggle or woo.
For in life's funny play, where memes intertwine,
We find meaning's shadow in laughter's design!

## Beyond the Surface

In a world of hashtags and likes,
We ponder the depth of our spikes.
Is a moment defined by a meme,
Or is life more than just a dream?

Scroll through excuses and quick-witted jests,
Glimpse of the truth hides in quests.
Between selfies and coffee so fine,
We yearn for a purpose divine.

Yet laughter bubbles in every shared post,
A giggle, a snort, we cherish the most.
Funny faces, oh how they uplift,
In the cereal bowl, there's wisdom adrift.

So let's dance in the chaos of scrolls,
Embrace the absurd with all of our souls.
For a meme might just spark that bright light,
Making nonsense feel perfectly right.

## The Quest for Context

In a sea of remarks that collide,
What treasure lies deep, can we decide?
For each witty quip hides a story,
Between context and chaos, we find glory.

Puns and pranks make our spirits soar,
Yet some nod and ponder, demanding more.
Is context a king or a mere passing bard,
In this world that seems mostly absurd?

Together we laugh at our shared confusion,
In a whirlpool of memes, a grand illusion.
What's the meaning? Ask your pet cat!
Or simply embrace the playful spat.

So let's seek the signs, the art of the jest,
With a wink and a smile, go on, be our best.
For laughter's the key that opens the door,
In the land of the lost, it's what we adore.

## Masks of Meaning

Shiny masks made of fiber and flair,
Hide the thoughts we all silence with care.
Behind every smile lies a mystery,
What's accurate? Let's make it a history!

With every joke shared on a timeline so grand,
We paint over edges with a meme in our hand.
But peek through the laughter, a shadow does dance,
Is it depth or just another meme chance?

So here we are in a maze of disguise,
Riddles and puns – oh how time flies!
Is it fluff or is it solid gold?
Every retweet whispers stories untold.

As we parade through the pixels, we seek,
Not ultimate answers, but only a peek.
To lift up the masks, and just have a laugh,
In this tangled web, let joy be our path.

## Ecstasy in Ephemerality

Moments drift like clouds in the breeze,
Fleeting shadows make mischief with ease.
We catch laughter in a paper-thin cup,
But hold on tight, for they fade and erupt.

In snapshots and memes our worlds collide,
Quick tastes of joy that we can't abide.
Do they spark joy, or just tickle the mind?
As we search for the gem that's well-defined.

Yet each fleeting snicker we hoard like gold,
In a vault of absurdity, brave and bold.
For a smile's a treasure, forever it blooms,
In the absurdity of these all-too-short rooms.

So, embrace the silly, let spontaneity reign,
In the blur of the quick, the joy and the pain.
For life's just a meme that we share in delight,
In the dance of existence, everything's light!

## Threads of Thought

In the web of our minds, thoughts tangle and play,
Like kittens with yarn, they scatter away.
We muse over meaning, but memes steal the show,
As laughter erupts from the seeds we sow.

A philosopher's brow is furrowed in doubt,
While TikTokers laugh and just dance it out.
Contemplation is grand, yet it's hard to ignore,
The cat memes that conquer, we all can't restore.

Wisdom's a riddle, that's cleverly spun,
But a meme with a cat? Now that's really fun!
We ponder existence, then scroll through the feed,
Is life meant for thinking, or just meant to meme?

From rants on existence to videos of fails,
We toggle between depth and entertaining tales.
If laughter's the answer, then what was the quest?
Threads of our thoughts might just need a rest!

## The Irony of Insight

The deepest of thinkers, with glasses askew,
Tripped over insights, and what did they view?
A pet video viral, with fish doing tricks,
Turns wisdom to folly, our minds in the mix.

Pondering meaning by candlelight glow,
They accidentally click, now it's chaos below.
The irony's thick, as deep thoughts fall flat,
While trends on the internet make us all laugh at that.

With charts and equations, they search for the key,
Yet a meme of a sloth brings them to glee.
Philosophers chuckle, they can't help but grin,
As priorities shift, and the laughter begins.

So here's to the wit found in spaces absurd,
Where memes teach us lessons without needing words.
From insight to irony, we dance on the rim,
Is wisdom the journey, or just having a whim?

# Chronicles of Comedy

In tales of existence, we laugh and we sigh,
With punchlines of meaning that soar to the sky.
Chronicles written on walls with bright hues,
A saga of mishaps and viral good news.

Life's but a comedy, can't we all see?
With characters chasing a joke by the sea.
Philosophers laugh 'til they roll on the floor,
While memes round the globe make you come back for more.

Echoes of jest in the halls of the wise,
A meme here and there? Oh, it's quite the surprise!
We ponder and wonder, yet in all the mess,
A chuckle and giggle bring some happiness.

So pen down your thoughts, let the laughter ignite,
In chronicles crafted of humor and light.
Where life's grand debate is a flash on the screen,
And meaning or meme? Well, it's all in between!

## **Echoes of Enigma**

What is the purpose, we scratch at our heads,
As we follow the memes that dance up ahead.
Is life a deep mystery or just one big joke?
With puns and good giggles, we leave them bespoke.

In the hall of confusion, with laughs all around,
Wisdom gets wedged in a viral sound.
A sage with a beard, and a cat on his lap,
Proclaiming the meaning while snoring a nap.

The jokes that we tell are the truths that we seek,
Yet wisdom feels fragile, in chaos we peek.
The echoes of enigma, so funny yet deep,
In memes we confide and in laughter, we reap.

So let's toast to the puzzle of life and its layers,
Where humor's our teacher and wisdom's a player.
In echoes we find both the jest and the glean,
As we dance through the whims, in this grand, silly scene!

## The Sigh of Subtlety

In a world where memes flicker,
The wise ones often snicker.
Is life a joke or a jest?
Let's laugh and ponder the quest.

With hashtags bright and clever,
We chase the trends forever.
Do wise thoughts wear funny hats?
Or is the truth in laughing cats?

Philosophers wield their quips,
While logic does a few flips.
The punchline lands with a thud,
As deep thoughts swim in a flood.

So take a seat and be amused,
By life's strange quirks, we're bemused.
With every meme, a chuckle's due,
Finding meaning's not so taboo.

## **Laughter's Legacy**

Laughter bounces off the walls,
Echoing through our joyful halls.
In moments small, we find our cheer,
With puns and gags that endear.

Is wisdom wrapped in punchlines tight?
Or does humor obscure the light?
With each bright meme that seems so sly,
We ponder truth in a winked eye.

Life's absurdities we embrace,
With playful jests we find our grace.
The legacy of laughter's call,
Turns solemn frowns to silly brawls.

So giggle through the cosmic dance,
As irony gives us a chance.
In jest, we seek the profound truth,
While memes bring joy to our youth.

## Unraveling the Paradox

A paradox wrapped in a joke,
Is this life's way to provoke?
With irony as our silly guide,
We trot along the meme-filled ride.

Philosophers scratch their heads,
While we giggle in our beds.
The search for meaning feels so grand,
Yet memes fit snug within our hands.

Does depth reside in laughter's wave?
Or in the memes that we all save?
As giggles bloom like flowers bright,
We chase the shadows of insight.

So here's to laughter, sharp and bold,
In every punchline, truth is told.
Through funny faces, we might see,
The depths of life, absurdity.

## Smile as Substance

A smile, a meme, both seem the same,
In this grand circus of life's game.
With chocolate cake and silly hats,
We ponder meaning with friendly chats.

Is wisdom found in a funny quirk?
Or does truth hide in the smirk?
With laughter dripping like sweet cream,
We chase the echoes of our dream.

In digital realms, we swipe and share,
Absurdity dances in the air.
Smiles, like memes, become our guide,
As we unfold what's deep inside.

So raise a glass to giggles bright,
To every meme that brings delight.
In smiles and laughter, we will find,
The meaning that's lovingly entwined.

## The Echo of a Laugh

In a world of jest and play,
We ponder the meaning day by day.
A punchline drops, and then we see,
Is laughter the key, or just a meme?

Faces in fits, they bend and sway,
Life's a joke, or so they say.
Wisdom wrapped in a giggle's glow,
Or maybe just a viral show?

With every chuckle that fills the air,
We search for answers, unaware.
Is the giggle sage, the sage a clown?
Or do we all just wear a crown?

So here's to laughter, the silliest quest,
Finding meaning in jest, we're truly blessed.
In every snort and silly wheeze,
We might just find life's missing keys!

**Irony in Intent**

Searching for purpose in a cat's cool stare,
We scroll through memes, thinking we care.
Between the giggles, truth may reside,
But irony lives right by our side.

A scholar's quote meets a duck face grin,
Intentions clear - or lost in spin?
The overlords of laughter take their throne,
While seekers roam, forever alone.

Bold proclamations wrapped in jokes,
Are we wise fools, or just clever folks?
With every meme, our thoughts entwined,
In a world of chaos, what have we mined?

Let's raise a toast to the irony found,
In the depths of humor, where truth abounds.
With every chuckle, we light the way,
Through absurdity's lens, we seize the day!

## Meaning Behind the Meme

Peering closely at the pixelated frames,
We search for meaning beyond the games.
Is it wisdom or just a passing trend?
In every image, do hints extend?

The doge smiles; the cat winks sly,
But what's the wisdom that makes us sigh?
Behind each viral musing, do we find,
A treasure chest of thoughts combined?

A screenshot taken, a truth confined,
Wrapped in laughter, it's redefined.
In colors bright, life's facts collide,
The depth of thought, we often hide.

So let's decode this silly spree,
Finding pearls in the absurdity.
For every meme holds a cosmic key,
Unlocking understanding, wild and free!

**Joyful Inquiries**

Why do we giggle when life turns grim?
Searching for answers, our chances slim.
In quirky dances and playful grins,
We ask life's questions through silly spins.

Do memes bring solace, or just a smile?
Are we laughing at life's chaotic style?
With every chuckle, we ponder the lore,
Is there meaning behind each roar?

In joyous inquiries, we seek delight,
Wading through nonsense, we take flight.
With smiles and memes as our trusty guides,
We ride the waves of life's silly tides.

So raise your glass to the jests we share,
In this dance of life, we lose our care.
With laughter and memes, let's find our way,
In joyful inquiries, let's seize the day!

## Shadows of Satire

In gardens of jest, truths often bloom,
While laughter erupts from the depths of gloom.
A dance of the quirks, a circus of thought,
Who knew nonsense could be so dearly sought?

Philosophers ponder in slippers and hats,
Seeking wisdom in the meows of the cats.
With winks and with giggles, the world spins around,
In the carnival chaos, meaning's not found.

A barrel of monkeys, they say, leads the way,
To secrets of life that we often betray.
So, slide down the banister of absurdity's glee,
Where the shadows of satire paint life's own decree.

Why fret over purpose when punchlines exist?
With each goofy jest, unnoticed we twist.
The truths are like clowns in this grand mystery,
Playing hide and seek with our history's glee.

## The Seriousness of Silly

In a world of the wise, the silly shines bright,
With giggles and gags taking center stage light.
The serious folks scribble their thoughts with a pen,
While the jesters just chuckle and plot their next skit.

With wisdom on pause, they throw cream pies wide,
And reason takes cover on this merry ride.
How profound is a stumble, how wise is a fall?
When silliness reigns, echoes laughter for all.

A riddle wrapped in rhymes, oh what a tease,
As jests mingle with logic, like honey with cheese.
Life's caught in this loop of ridiculous schemes,
Where nonsense writes novels and logic just dreams.

So bring out the juggler with dreams in his eyes,
Embrace all the madness—no need for goodbyes.
With humor as armor, we wade through the fray,
For the seriousness of silly keeps worries at bay.

## Searching for Significance

With magnifying glasses and maps made of cheese,
We wander the world trying hard to appease.
In search of a meaning, we trip on our toes,
While mystery giggles as our sanity goes.

Doodles of depth fill our notebooks with haste,
But infamy looms at the end of the chase.
Perhaps it's a sandwich or maybe a cat,
That holds all the answers we're desperately at.

The wise sage with cookies, he nudges our dreams,
As meaning's a puzzle made up of, it seems—
A riddle of quirks and a basket of laughs,
Like life's a math problem solved by its halves.

So toast to the fun and the questions we weave,
In the tapestry of life, let's laugh and believe.
For while we keep searching, let's loosen the tie,
And relish the ride with a chuckle, oh my!

## Hidden Gems in Guffaws

Amongst the jests lies a treasure so bright,
In laughter's embrace, the day turns to night.
A wink and a giggle, oh what a delight,
As wisdom hides shyly, just out of our sight.

With tickles and snickers, our minds start to churn,
The sparkles of silliness, how they brightly burn.
Searching for answers in gales of good cheer,
Each guffaw a gem that the wise hold so dear.

In banters and chuckles, truths start to emerge,
With slapstick philosophy—a joyous surge.
Like squirrels with nuts, we gather these laughs,
Each punchline a clue on our whimsical paths.

So dig through the humor and find what you seek,
In the playground of nonsense, the brave hearts will peek.

For hidden gems spark in the chaos of jest,
And life's true meaning lies where joy knows best.

www.ingramcontent.com/pod-product-compliance
Lightning Source LLC
Chambersburg PA
CBHW071852160426
43209CB00003B/518